TINY THINGS BIG IMPACTS

BEES

Written By John Wood

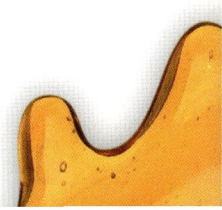

BookLife
PUBLISHING

©2018
BookLife Publishing
King's Lynn
Norfolk PE30 4LS

All rights reserved.
Printed in Malaysia.

A catalogue record for this book is available from the British Library.

ISBN: 978-1-78637-422-6

Written by:
John Wood

Edited by:
Holly Duhig

Designed by:
Amy Li

All facts, statistics, web addresses and URLs in this book were verified as valid and accurate at time of writing. No responsibility for any changes to external websites or references can be accepted by either the author or publisher.

PHOTO CREDITS

All images are courtesy of Shutterstock.com, unless stated otherwise.

Cover – BEAUTYTHIN, COLOA Studio, Daniel Prudek, jukurae, Borders & Bees – BEAUTYTHIN, COLOA Studio, world of vector, 1 – Daniel Prudek, jukurae, 4–5 – Magdalenawd, GoncharukMaks, phive, Kuttelvaserova Stuchelova, 6 – Kosmos111, pukach, 7 – Aron M, treesak, 8 – STILLFX, Here, jesuspereia, sraphotohut, 9 – Andrea Izzotti, djile, 10 – windwalk, Ollyy, solomon7, Korionov, Humannet Macrovector, 11 – CLAYTON ANDERSEN, Dmitri Gomon, 12 – Feng Yu, Rolf G Wackenberg, Africa Studio, 13 – Jeffrey Schwartz, Anamania Mejia, Paul Richard Jones, NataliaNM, 14 – Hector Sanchez, Here, Runrun2, STILLFX, Vorim, 15 – ANTONIO TRUZZI, artajazz, Dani Vincek, Fleur_de_papier, Goskova Tatiana, olodymyr Krasyuk, 16 – Yuri samsonov, Pavlo S, guteksk7, 17 – Caitlin Petolea, AlessandraRC, 18 – pokkate, Jiri Hera, TorriPhoto, 19 – bigacis, Lotus Images, Toii Scape, Khumthong, 20 – MicroOne, stockish, Ttatty, 21 – Angelina Babii, Ian Dyball, 22 – Africa Studio, Gts, DenisProduction.com, 23 – Chuck Wagner, gyn9037, Tetiana Rostopira, 24 – Fleur_de_papier, macondo, WKanadapon, Ollyy, 25 – Pigprox, Chutima Chaochaiya, 26 – Darios, Lampas Azami, 27 – Oleksandrum, Fotokostic, 28 – Kuttlevaserova Stuchelova, Photografiero, Mirko Graul

BEES

CONTENTS:

Page 4	Meet the Honey Bee
Page 6	A World Without Bees
Page 8	The Last Jar of Honey
Page 10	Empty Supermarket Shelves
Page 12	Ice Cream Shortage
Page 14	Meat Costs More
Page 16	No More Almonds
Page 18	New Cake Recipes
Page 20	Cosmetics
Page 22	Rare Jeans
Page 24	Finding a New Job
Page 26	Threats to Bees
Page 30	Saving the Bees
Page 31	Glossary
Page 32	Index

WORDS THAT LOOK LIKE THIS ARE EXPLAINED IN THE GLOSSARY ON PAGE 31.

MEET THE HONEY BEE

This is a honey bee. A honey bee worker is around 10–15 millimetres long. Like many other insects, it has six legs, a pair of wings and two antennae on its head. However, unlike many other insects, these little honey bees change the world every day. They might seem small and unimportant, but without them our lives would be very different indeed.

The Three Bees

There are three different types of bees. Worker bees are the smallest, and it is their job to collect food for the hive. The queen bee is the mother of the hive, and she gives birth to all the young. Drone bees **mate** with the queen.

HONEY BEES LIVE IN A HIVE.

Queen Bee

Drone Bee

Honey Makes the World Go Round

Worker honey bees have an important mission: to make as much honey as possible. The hive needs to be full of honey because that is mostly what bees eat.

Each day, honey bees leave their home to visit as many flowers as they can. At each flower, they collect a type of sugar called nectar, which they store in their stomachs. Once they are full, they make their way back to the hive. Here, they will chew the nectar until it turns into honey.

It takes 12 bees all their lives to make a single teaspoon of honey.

Honey is stored in honeycomb.

Honeycomb

Worker Bee

A WORLD WITHOUT BEES

This bee has got pollen on its face.

Why Are Bees so Important?

Plants and flowers grow from seeds. To make seeds, most flowers need to swap **pollen** with each other. To do this, they rely on bees. As bees visit the flowers for nectar, they are covered with sticky pollen. They accidentally carry this pollen to the next flower. The pollen gets stuck to the new flower, and new seeds can be made. This is called pollination.

Insects that carry pollen, such as bees, are called pollinators.

HONEY BEES WILL TRAVEL AS FAR AS 12 KILOMETRES AWAY FROM THE HIVE TO FIND FLOWERS..

Without pollinators, many types of flowering plants would not be able to make seeds, and so there would be no new flowers. Lots of plants would die out.

Bees are very useful pollinators all over the world. Honey bees pollinate more **crops** than any other creature. Honey bee hives are transported to lots of different farms in big trucks. Then, they are released to pollinate the plants.

Honey bees pollinate more than 80% of the crops grown in the US.

HONEY BEES HAVE TO VISIT AROUND 5 MILLION FLOWERS TO MAKE AROUND 560 MILLILITRES OF HONEY.

Bye-Bye, Bees

If all the bees disappeared tomorrow, nobody knows what would happen for sure. Maybe humans would find a way to replace bees and solve all the problems. But what if we couldn't?

Throughout this book, we are going to take a look at what might happen in a world without bees.

THE LAST JAR OF HONEY

BREAKING NEWS: THE LAST JAR OF HONEY WAS SOLD TODAY, AT 11:15 AM. OUR REPORTER, MR SCASE, IS ON THE SCENE.

"Thank you. Yes, since the disappearance of honey bees, we all knew this day would come. There is no more honey left. I'm here with Mr Liddington, a shopper who was just too late. How are you feeling, Mr Liddington?"

TERRIBLE! NOW WHAT WILL I PUT ON MY TOAST?!

How Do We Get Honey from Bees?

Most honey bees are not wild – they are kept by people called beekeepers. Bees make extra honey for the winter, when there are no flowers or nectar. Beekeepers use honey bees because these bees make an especially large amount of extra honey.

Beekeepers sell the extra honey, but they leave enough so that the bees have plenty to eat during winter.

A Beekeeper Collecting Honey

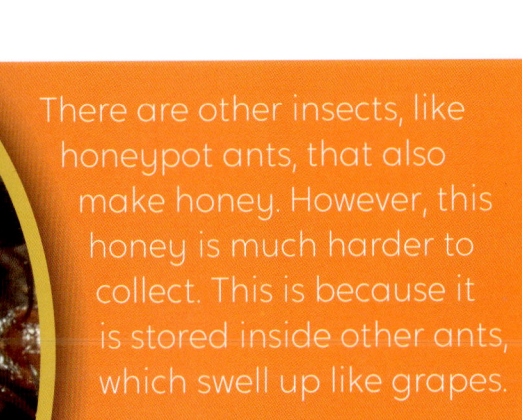

There are other insects, like honeypot ants, that also make honey. However, this honey is much harder to collect. This is because it is stored inside other ants, which swell up like grapes.

Honeypot Ants

EMPTY
SUPERMARKET SHELVES

Whole Foods

For a short time in 2013, a supermarket called Whole Foods stopped selling all the food that needed pollinators in one of its shops. This was done to teach people about the importance of bees. As well as other foods mentioned on this page, lemons, limes, carrots and broccoli were also taken off the shelves.

237 products out of 453 were taken off the shelves in one Whole Foods.

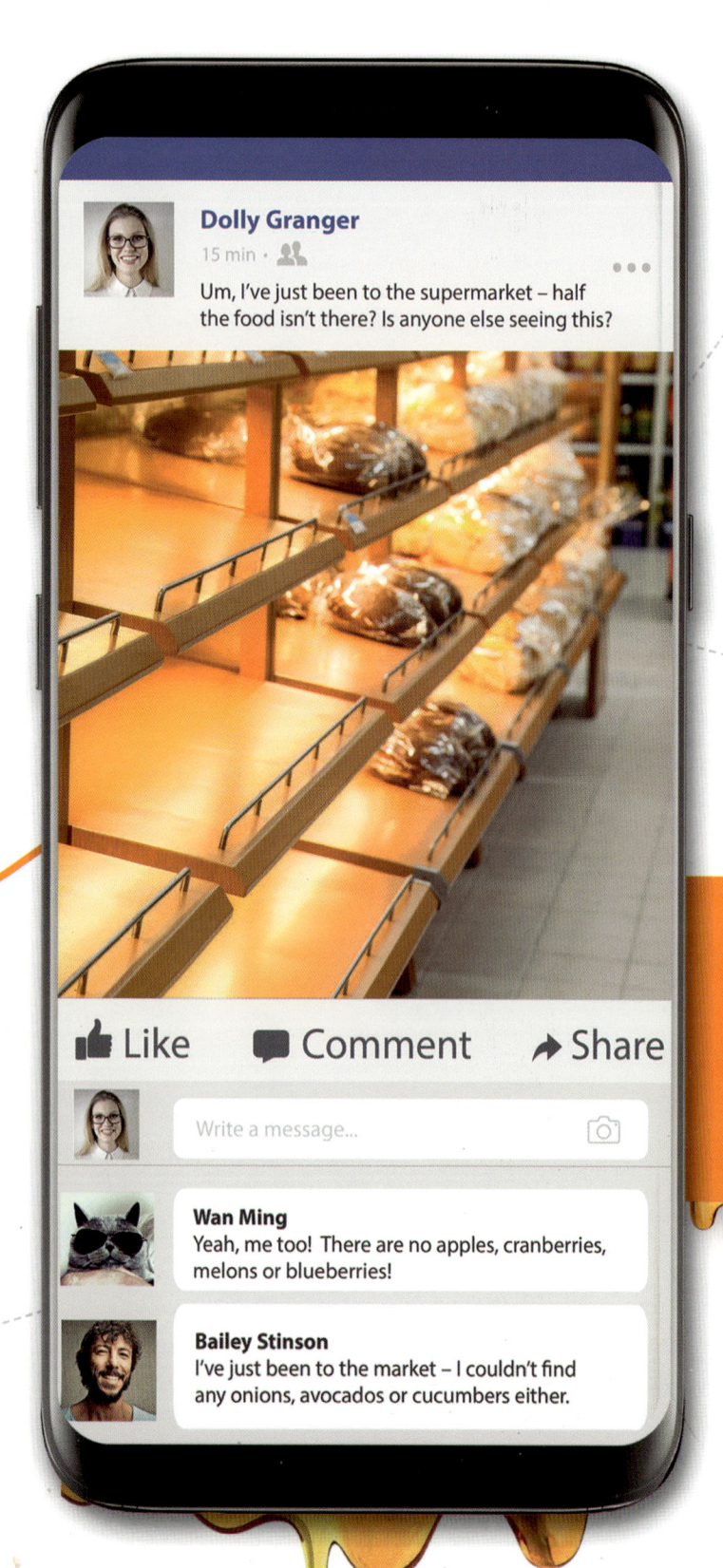

Dolly Granger
15 min

Um, I've just been to the supermarket – half the food isn't there? Is anyone else seeing this?

Like   Comment   Share

Write a message...

Wan Ming
Yeah, me too! There are no apples, cranberries, melons or blueberries!

Bailey Stinson
I've just been to the market – I couldn't find any onions, avocados or cucumbers either.

Butterfly

Pollinators Needed!

Many insects can also be pollinators, although bees are the best. Ants are pollinators, but most do not have wings, so they can only pollinate plants close to the ground. Some ants are also covered with a **substance** that protects them against **infections** but also destroys pollen. Butterflies are also pollinators, but because of their long thin legs, they do not catch much pollen on their bodies.

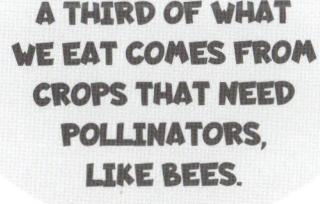

> A THIRD OF WHAT WE EAT COMES FROM CROPS THAT NEED POLLINATORS, LIKE BEES.

Honey bees pollinate 80% of the crops we eat. Without bees, people would have to make do with whatever fruits and vegetables the shops could find.

Whether they are wild or kept by bee keepers, bees are the most important pollinators.

ICE CREAM
SHORTAGE

DAILY NEWS

WORLDWIDE ICE CREAM SHORTAGE

Children say 'enough is enough'.

By J. Pointer

Shops are no longer selling ice cream, as they are missing the main ingredient: milk. Scientists have said that it's all because there are no bees left to pollinate the cow's food. Since there isn't enough milk, ice cream factories have been forced to close down until the problem has been solved.

Children across the world are feeling the effects. Tantrums have been reported across the world, especially with summer coming. Ice cream vans around the globe have been travelling to the World Ice Cream Van Summit to discuss what to do next. Locals say the noise has been horrendous, as the jingles of thousands of vans mix together.

Ice cream shops all around the world are closed down.

This reporter travelled to Yorkshire, England, which has the third-largest ice cream factory. In an interview with a factory worker, he said "There'll be no milkshakes next, mark my words. Then we'll be in real trouble."

More on Page 10.

Missing Milk

In a world without bees, milk might become rarer or more **expensive**. This will also happen to things made out of milk, like cheese, yoghurt and cream. It also affects ice cream, because ice cream is made from milk (and lots and lots of sugar).

How Do Bees Help Us Get Milk?

We get milk from cows. We feed cows lots of things which have been crushed up. However, most of a cow's food comes from plants such as alfalfa and clover. Like many plants, the alfalfa and clover plants need to be pollinated, and this is mostly done by bees.

Red Clover

Alfalfa

ALFALFA IS OFTEN DRIED AND MADE INTO HAY.

Cows eat around 2% of their body weight every day. This is around 12 kilograms of food a day.

Less cow food means fewer cows. Cows that are underfed are not healthy, and make much less milk. It can also be harder for the cow to have babies.

MEAT
COSTS MORE

"... And now, the news. Beef has become much more expensive this week, as meat becomes rarer and rarer. Most families can no longer afford things like steak or beef mince. Some foods, like burgers and spaghetti bolognese, might become a treat which people have once a year. This is one of many problems since the Great Bee Disappearance..."

Without the alfalfa and clover that the bees pollinate, there will be fewer cows. This means there would be less meat in the shops, especially beef, as beef comes from cows.

ALFALFA IS EATEN BY ALL SORTS OF FARM ANIMALS, INCLUDING SHEEP AND PIGS.

Why Would Meat Become Expensive?

The reason meat prices would go up is because beef would become rarer. When something becomes rare, it means that it can't be shared between everyone. Rich people would pay more because they really want the beef and can afford to buy it. This means the seller can sell the meat for a much higher price.

Without bees, beef might become unavailable, no matter where you shop or how much you pay.

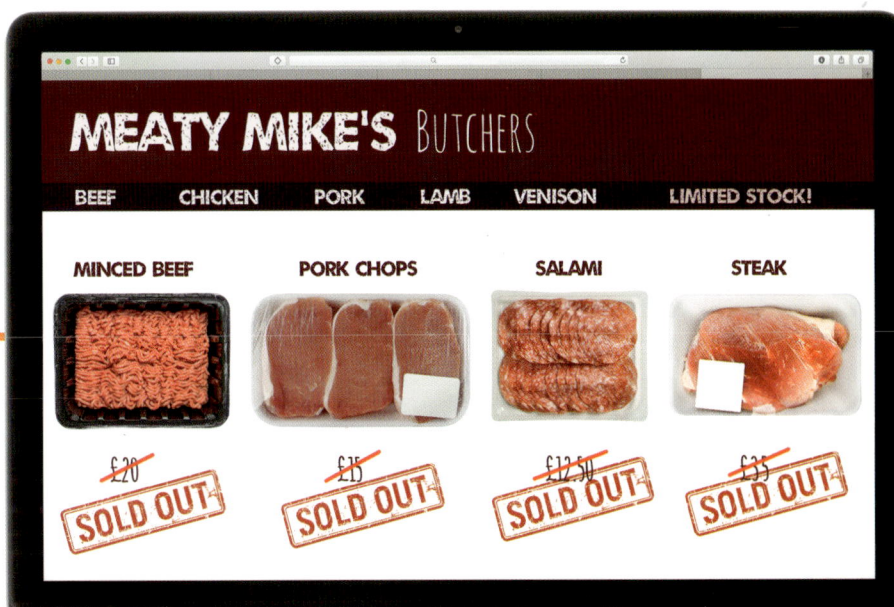

People are willing to pay more money for rare things. Things made of gold are more expensive because gold is a rare metal. Burgers full of beef would become expensive for the same reason.

THE ONION, CHEESE, BEEF AND BACON IN THIS IMAGE MIGHT NOT BE EASILY AVAILABLE IN A WORLD WITHOUT BEES.

NO MORE ALMONDS

Text message conversation:

- I'm going to the shop tonight, is there anything you want?
- Almond Milk!
- There are no almonds anymore, remember? The bees have all gone.
- Marzipan!
- That's made out of almonds.
- Almond Cake!
- Seriously?? There are no more almonds! I'll get you some bananas instead.
- :(

What Is an Almond?

Almonds are a type of seed. They can be eaten as a snack, ground up to make milk or oil, or used as an **ingredient** in other types of food, such as cereal, marzipan and chocolate.

Almonds are healthy. In one study, scientists named almonds as one of the most nutritious foods.

Almonds

80% of the world's almonds come from California, in the USA. As more people around the world wanted almonds, more almond **orchards** were planted. However, there are no longer enough bees in California to pollinate all these almond orchards, so they have to borrow bees from all around the country.

An Almond Orchard in California

AROUND 30 BILLION BEES TRAVEL FROM AROUND AMERICA TO HELP CALIFORNIAN BEES POLLINATE THE ALMOND ORCHARDS.

Bees on Wheels

Some trucks that carry bee hives can be driving for up to three days. The truck has to keep moving all the time so the bees stay still. A giant net is also used to keep the bees inside.

NEW CAKE RECIPES

Cauliflower Cake

The best thing about this cake recipe is that there is no butter or oil in it, as well as nothing made from milk. This is a good thing because, since the Great Bee Disappearance, you might not have these things lying around the house anymore.

If at first it tastes a little bit like paper, don't worry! This is normal.

Ingredients:
2 Cauliflowers
4 Large Eggs
240g Plain Flour
1tsp Baking Powder
240g Sugar
½ tsp Salt

Sunflowers

Lots of food, like cake, contains butter and oil. Most butter is made from milk, or nuts and seeds such as almonds. A lot of oil is made from coconuts or plants such as rapeseed and sunflowers.

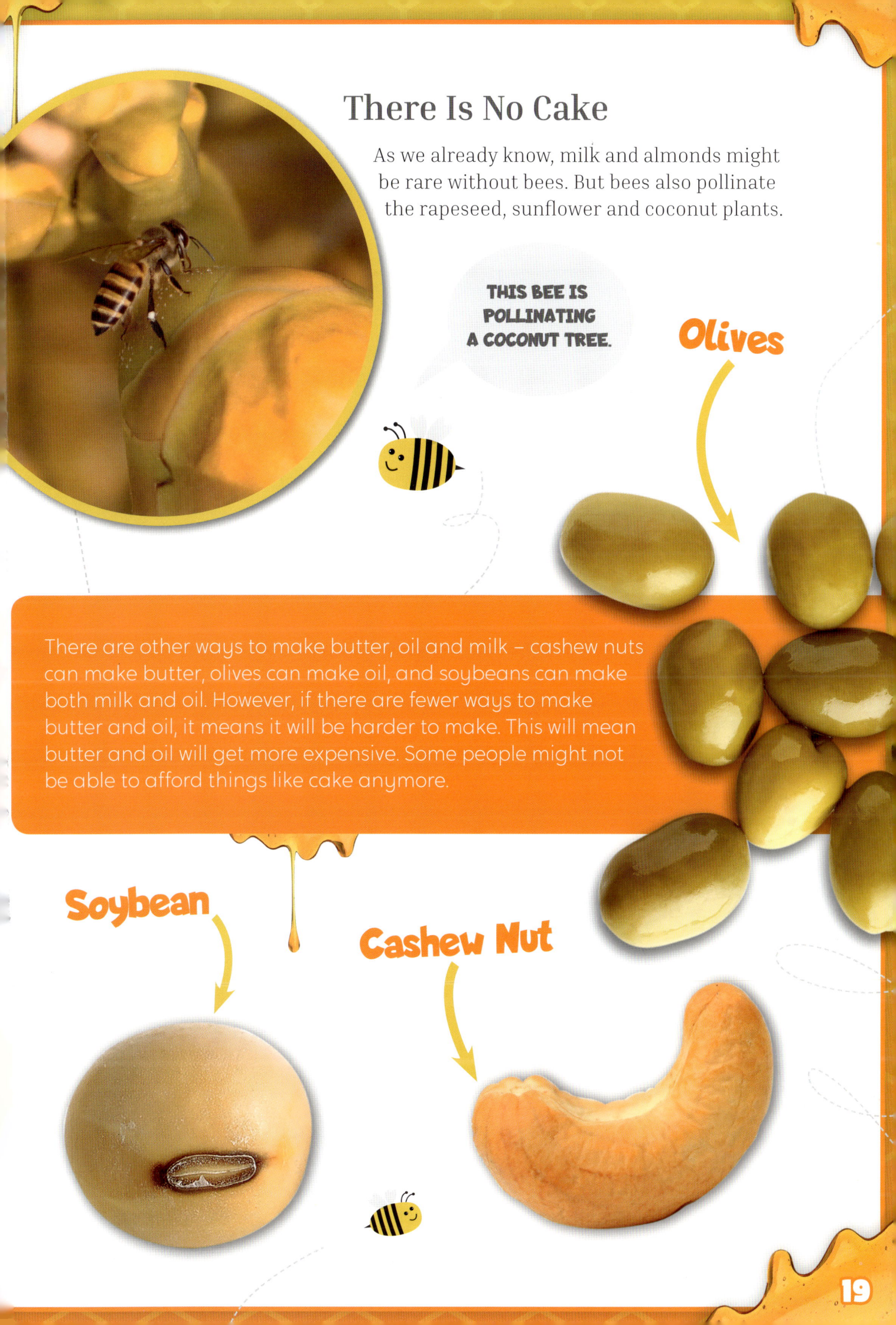

There Is No Cake

As we already know, milk and almonds might be rare without bees. But bees also pollinate the rapeseed, sunflower and coconut plants.

THIS BEE IS POLLINATING A COCONUT TREE.

Olives

There are other ways to make butter, oil and milk – cashew nuts can make butter, olives can make oil, and soybeans can make both milk and oil. However, if there are fewer ways to make butter and oil, it means it will be harder to make. This will mean butter and oil will get more expensive. Some people might not be able to afford things like cake anymore.

Soybean

Cashew Nut

COSMETICS

New message

To: you@email.co.uk
Subject: Your order has been cancelled

Dear Customer,

I want to say sorry. You ordered some things online from us, but they are now unavailable.
Here is a list of what you ordered:

- Skin Moisturiser
- Hair Conditioner
- Face Wash

We no longer sell these things because they need bees. Unfortunately, as you know, there are no bees left.
We will let you know when we've solved this problem. If you see any bees in the meantime, please let me know!

Best regards,

Maddie

(Owner of the big supermarket down the road)

Send

Cosmetics

Cosmetics are things which are used on the face or in hair for health or beauty reasons. Bees make honey and wax, which are both used a lot in cosmetics.

Beeswax

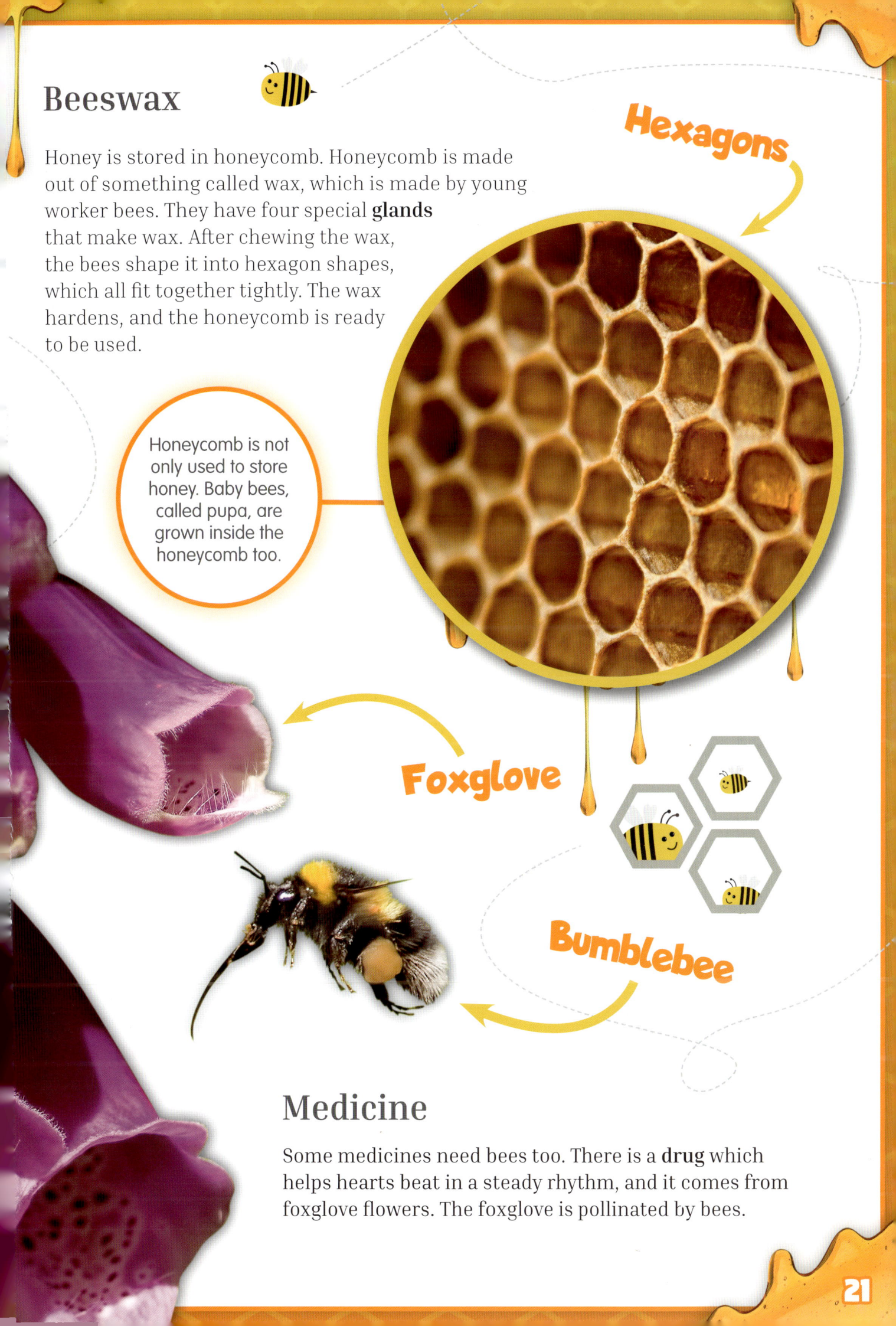

Honey is stored in honeycomb. Honeycomb is made out of something called wax, which is made by young worker bees. They have four special **glands** that make wax. After chewing the wax, the bees shape it into hexagon shapes, which all fit together tightly. The wax hardens, and the honeycomb is ready to be used.

Honeycomb is not only used to store honey. Baby bees, called pupa, are grown inside the honeycomb too.

Hexagons

Foxglove

Bumblebee

Medicine

Some medicines need bees too. There is a **drug** which helps hearts beat in a steady rhythm, and it comes from foxglove flowers. The foxglove is pollinated by bees.

RARE JEANS

beebay

search

For Sale: Pair of Jeans, RARE!

Price: £300

Condition: Used

Seller: Kelbdog

I'm selling my last pair of jeans because they don't fit me anymore. They are dark blue and don't have any holes in.

Since the bees disappeared, you don't see that many jeans around now. That makes this pair quite special! Message me if you are interested.
No time-wasters.

Clothes and More

Without bees, things like bedsheets, teabags, towels, bandages and many clothes might cost more money, or become rarer. This is because these things are all made out of cotton.

> YOU ARE PROBABLY WEARING CLOTHES MADE OUT OF COTTON RIGHT NOW.

Cotton Plant

What Is Cotton?

Cotton is a type of **fibre** that comes from a plant. Cotton plants are pollinated by many insects, but mainly bees. The fibres are usually picked, cleaned, combed and then spun into **yarn** by machines.

Cotton seed oil is sometimes used when making soap, margarine, rubber and plastic.

Once the cotton has been spun into long threads, it can be made into all sorts of things. When the threads are put together in a special way, it can make a strong material called denim. This is what jeans are made from.

A Machine Weaving Cotton

COTTON IS VERY IMPORTANT, AND SO ARE THE BEES.

23

FINDING A NEW JOB

Fewer Jobs

Millions and millions of people have jobs that wouldn't exist without bees. Beekeepers and farmers who own cows or certain crops would lose their jobs. People who make clothes or cosmetics that need bees might not be able to go to work.

buzzer

Kirsty the Beekeeper
@Kirstybee

The hives are empty. This is NOT GOOD for a beekeeper. I think this means I don't have a job anymore…
#FindTheBees #NoHoneyNoMoney #WeMissTheSoundOfBuzzing

299,792,458 Retweets   **101,542,899** Likes

Reply to @Kirstybee

IT CAN SOMETIMES BE HARD TO GET A NEW JOB.

Without jobs, people might not be able to feed themselves or their families. All around the world, many people might struggle to look after themselves, keep their homes and stay healthy.

Money

When people buy and sell things with each other, it is called trading. Trade is good, and it makes everyone richer. However, if bees disappeared, there would be much less trade because people would have fewer things to buy and sell.

Every year, between £28 billion and £68 billion is made thanks to the bees pollinating plants.

THREATS
TO BEES

A future without bees looks very scary indeed. However, in today's world, bees are in danger.

Many scientists and beekeepers have been worried in recent years. This is because bees seem to be dying out. Many millions of bees have disappeared, and there are many reasons why that could be.

90% OF POLLINATORS HAVE DISAPPEARED IN THE LAST 20 YEARS.

Colony Collapse Disorder

Colony Collapse Disorder (CCD) is a mysterious problem. All the bees in a hive disappear and don't come back, leaving the queen on her own. The bees are never found. This is a problem for beekeepers and the plants that need the bees for pollination.

Pesticides

Pesticides are a type of **chemical** that kill certain insects and plants. Some insects eat crops – these are known as pests, like the Colorado beetle who is known for eating potato crops. Some unwanted plants grow amongst the crops, and these are known as weeds. Pesticides kill pests and weeds. However, sometimes they accidentally kill bees too.

Colorado Beetle

From 2007 to 2013, more than 10 million bee hives have disappeared.

Most pesticides are spread by big companies who own lots of farms and crops.

Neonics

Neonicotinoids, or neonics for short, are a type of pesticide. They are used all over the world, and can be dangerous to bees. Some scientists think that neonics can stop bees being able to find their way home.

Disease

Other scientists have found that many hives with CCD also had a disease. The disease is called Israeli acute paralysis. It causes the wings to shiver, until eventually they can't move. This can kill many bees.

Parasites

A parasite is something that makes an animal sick by living on it. Parasites are usually very tiny creatures that suck blood or steal nutrients from much bigger animals. The varroa mite is a parasite of bees. It makes the bees sick and tired, and unable to collect enough food.

These varroa mites are living on young bees, which are called pupa.

Pupa

Driving around the Country

Some people think that bees are **stressed**. To pollinate lots of crops, honey bees are being driven all around the country. However, bees are not used to this – most bees live in a hive that stays still!

YOU'RE SO STRESSED, HONEY.

Is There One Reason?

Bees have a lot to worry about nowadays. There probably isn't one single reason why bees have been disappearing – it is probably lots of reasons all added up. However, there are things being done to save the bees.

SAVING
THE BEES

The **population** of honey bees kept by beekeepers is actually rising now. Some countries have **banned** some types of dangerous pesticides, too. This is good news, but people also need to remember that wild bees are still dying out.

IT IS IMPORTANT TO HAVE LOTS OF TYPES OF BEES, LIKE THIS WILD, RED-TAILED BUMBLEBEE.

What Can You Do to Help?

- Ask your parents to plant bee-friendly plants in the garden. Larkspur, flowering herbs, allium plants and even weeds are good.

- Write a letter to your local **MP** or council asking them to spend more money helping and protecting the bees.

- Talk about bees! Tell everyone that they are one of the most important little creatures in the world.

GLOSSARY

banned	when something isn't allowed
chemical	a substance that is usually produced artifically by scientists
crops	plants that are grown on a large scale because they are useful, usually as food
drug	a medicine or substance which has an effect on the body or mind
expensive	to costa lot of money
fibre	thread-like structures
glands	organs in the body which produce chemical substances for the body to use or get rid of
infections	illnesses caused by dirt, germs and bacteria getting into the body
ingredient	food items that are put together to make a particular meal
mate	to produce young with an animal of the same species
MP	member of parliament – the person elected to represent a local area in national government
nutritious	full of natural substances that animals and plants need to grow and stay healthy
orchards	groups of trees that are kept to grow fruit
pollen	a powder-like substance made by plants
population	the number of things living in a place
products	things that are made and usually sold in shops
stressed	being in a state of mental or emotional tension
substance	things with physical properties
yarn	thread that is ready for knitting, weaving or sewing

INDEX

almonds 16–19

animal 14, 28

ants 9, 11

beekeepers 9, 24, 26, 30

butter 18–19

clothes 22, 24

Colony Collapse Disorder (CCD) 26, 28

cotton 22–23

cows 13–14, 24

crops 7, 11, 24, 17, 29

disease 28

flowers 5–7, 9, 18–19, 21, 30

hive 4–7, 17, 26–29

honey 4–9, 11, 20, 19–30

honeycomb 5, 21

insects 4, 6, 9, 11, 23, 27

meat 14–15

medicine 21

milk 12–13, 16, 18–19

money 15, 22, 25, 30

nectar 5–6, 9

oil 16, 18–19, 23

pesticides 27, 30

plants 6–7, 11, 13, 17–19, 23, 25–27, 30

pollen 6, 11

pollinate 7, 11, 13–14, 17, 19, 21, 23, 29

seeds 6, 16, 18–19, 23

selling 10

vegetables 11

wax 20–21